help me
BECOME™

Becoming *A Good Spo*
Overcoming *Bad Spor*

mvpkids®

Block Bad
Sportsmanship™

SOPHIA DAY®

Written by Kayla Pearson   *Illustrated by* Timothy Zowada

The Sophia Day® Creative Team-

Kayla Pearson, Timothy Zowada, Stephanie Strouse,
Megan Johnson, Carol Sauder, Mel Sauder

A **special thank you** to our team of reviewers who graciously
give us feedback, edits and help ensure that our products
remain accurate, applicable and genuinely diverse.

Published and Distributed by MVP Kids Media, LLC -
Mesa, Arizona, USA
Printed by Prosperous Printing Inc. -
Shenzhen, China

Designed by Stephanie Strouse

DOM Jun 2019, Job # 03-010-01

May your childhood be filled with adventure, your days with hope and your learnings with wisdom, and may you continuously grow as an MVP Kid, preparing to lead a responsible, meaningful life.

-SOPHIA DAY

TABLE OF CONTENTS

Lucas' Picnic Games

Lucas and LeBron were excited for the Soaring Explorers' Picnic.

The day was packed full of fun and games. The Soaring Explorers split into three teams.

Arctic Wolves

The first game was the water balloon toss.
LeBron tossed the balloon to Lucas.
Lucas tossed the balloon to Wesley.

SPLAT! Wesley missed the balloon.
"Oh, come on, Wesley!" Lucas said, frustrated.
Their team was not off to a good start.

The next game didn't get better.

Neither did the game after that.

Wesley always seemed to make mistakes.

Lucas became **more** and **more**
frustrated. He said unkind things that
made Wesley want to quit the team.

Their group leader, Mr. Forrest, called Lucas aside for a talk. "I noticed you're getting upset. What's wrong?"

"Wesley is making us lose every game," said Lucas.

"Lucas, it's not about winning or losing. Focus on having fun with your friends."

"But Wesley keeps messing up,"
Lucas complained.

"Everyone makes mistakes.
Be a leader and help your team stay
positive. Work for the good of your pack, not
just for yourself."

"Like an
arctic wolf!"
Lucas exclaimed.

13

"Yes! They look out for each other. You can do the same. Instead of being hard on Wesley for his mistakes, encourage his strengths."

14

Lucas agreed to follow Mr. Forrest's advice. Before they started again, Lucas **apologized** to Wesley for not showing good sportsmanship.

In the next game, Lucas said
encouraging words to strengthen the pack.
They all worked hard together.

Lucas' team didn't win, but Lucas still **felt like a winner** for trying his best, encouraging his teammates and having a good time.

THINK & TALK ABOUT IT

Discuss the story...

1. How do you think Lucas felt when he first arrived at the picnic?

2. How did Lucas' attitude change when he started playing the games?

3. What did Lucas do that showed bad sportsmanship?

4. What did Mr. Forrest say was more important than winning or losing?

5. What happened when Lucas followed Mr. Forrest's advice?

Discuss how to apply the story...

1. What games do you like to play?

2. Good sportsmanship means to play fair while being kind to others. How do you show good sportsmanship when you play a game or sport?

3. When is it hard to be a good sport?

4. Why do you think teamwork is important?

5. What are some ways you can encourage your teammates?

FOR PARENTS & MENTORS: *Around age five is when children typically start to play to win and begin grasping a competitive attitude. Healthy competition can be a good thing, as it may challenge children to try harder and achieve new things. Unhealthy competition can leave kids feeling defeated. Model good sportsmanship in your home and teach that winning is not as important as effort and teamwork. Cooperative games and individual sports can help children who are too competitive because they focus on improving skills and teamwork rather than winning.*

Help prepare children for special events like the picnic in this story. Talk through what type of activities children can expect. State the appropriate behaviors and the consequences for poor behaviors. Practice skills for the games as well as communication skills needed for good teamwork.

For additional tips and reference information, visit **www.MVPkids.com**.

20

Miriam's Family Visit

Miriam's family from Egypt was coming to visit. Miriam couldn't wait to spend time with her cousins.

While they were visiting,
Miriam learned how to play
an ancient Egyptian game.

Miriam wasn't very good at first. She kept making mistakes and losing her pieces.

"I don't want to play. I quit!"

Miriam stomped away.

26

Aunt Aliaa followed Miriam into her room. "Miriam, you don't have to be perfect at everything you try."

"I can't stand making mistakes!"

"Making mistakes doesn't feel good. I don't like to lose either. But mistakes show that you are being brave and trying something new. As you learn from your mistakes, you'll get better."

"Do you remember what Grandfather always says?" asked Aunt Aliaa.

"Determination is the key to everything," answered Miriam.

"Yes. You can learn a lot from your mistakes if you don't quit."

"Tell me about a time you learned to do something that was difficult at first."

"You mean like reading?" Miriam remembered how hard it was to learn to read.

"Aren't you glad you didn't give up on reading? Now you love to read."

Aunt Aliaa was right. Miriam was glad she had worked so hard to read. She loved stories.

After talking with Aunt Aliaa, Miriam was determined to master the game. She carefully watched others play until she understood the strategy.

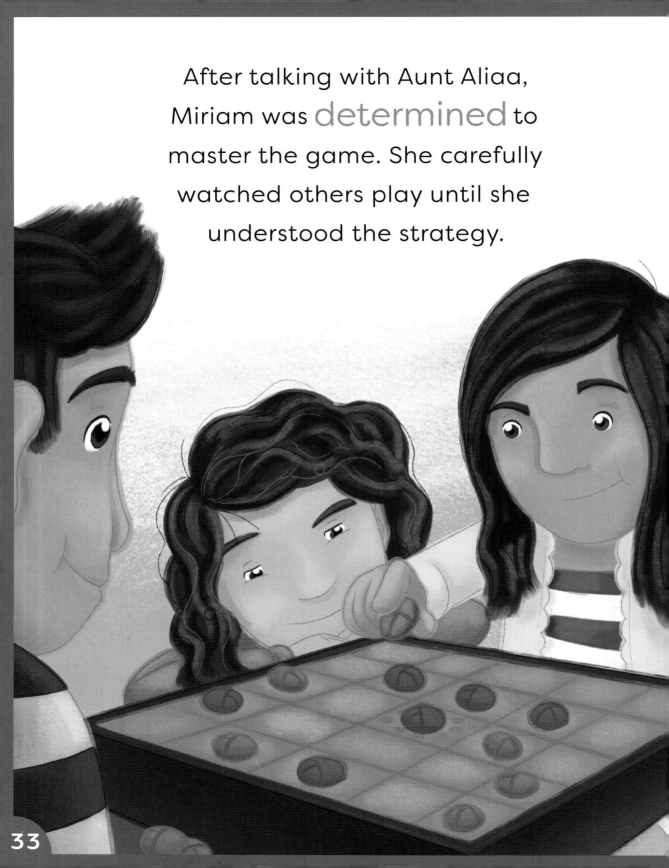

Miriam practiced patiently. After many tries, her determination helped her finally win!

"Way to go, Miriam!
You worked hard and figured it out.
Grandfather will be proud."

Miriam felt like
she could do anything
with her new determination.

It was a lot more fun to play with her family
than to quit and stomp away.

THINK & TALK ABOUT IT

Miriam's Family Visit

Discuss the story...

1. How did Miriam feel when she first tried to play the game?

2. What could Miriam have done instead of quitting the game?

3. What do you think "determination" means?

4. How did Miriam's attitude change after she talked with her Aunt Aliaa?

5. Do you think winning felt better to Miriam after she tried really hard? Why?

Discuss how to apply the story...

1. How do you feel when you lose a game?

2. What do you think you could do to improve at a game?

3. Do you think it is okay to make mistakes? Why?

4. What do you wish you could do that you can't do yet?

5. What can you do to accomplish that goal?

FOR PARENTS & MENTORS: *Games and sports are a great way to teach children important life lessons. Children can get easily discouraged if they make mistakes and lose a game. Use these moments to reframe negative thoughts and teach character traits such as determination and perseverance. If children make mistakes that cost them the game, help them problem-solve to see what to do differently the next time. Learning from mistakes can be the best motivation to improve skills. Take time reflecting together on things your child can do now that took them hard work to accomplish. Sharing stories of how you used determination in your life can inspire children. When children accomplish something new, praise them for their hard work and determination.*

Frankie's Baseball Game

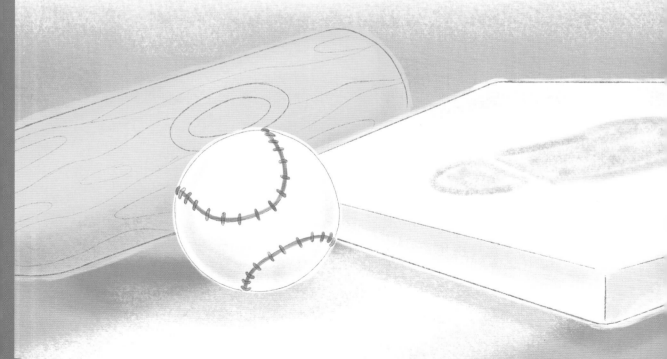

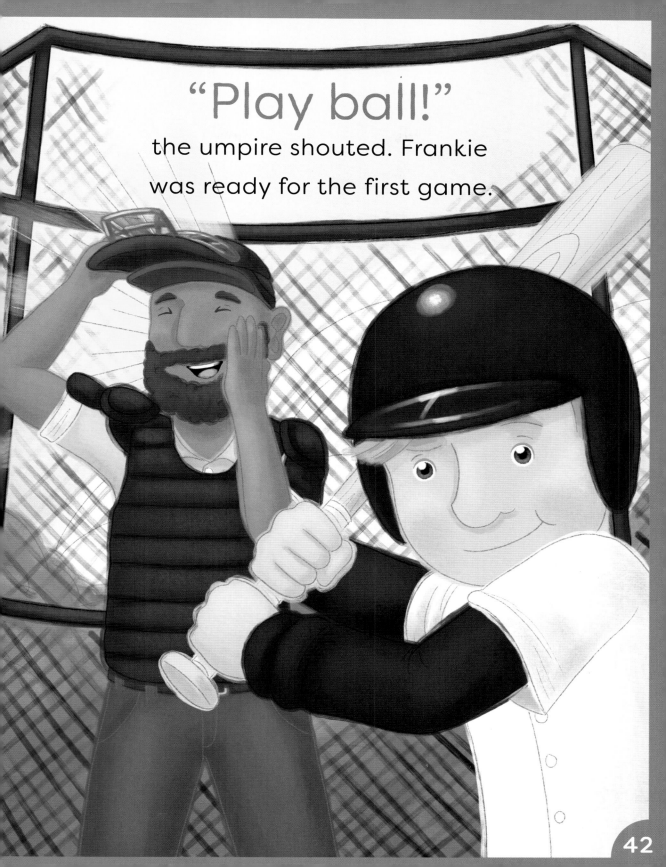

However, during the game, his teammate Jason was showing poor sportsmanship. He was saying mean things to his teammates, yelling at the umpire and taunting the other team.

44

Frankie knew this was disrespectful,
and he asked Jason to stop.

Jason didn't stop.
He was ruining the
fun for everyone.

46

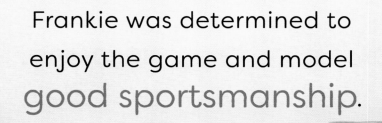

Frankie was determined to enjoy the game and model **good sportsmanship.**

He helped a player up who slid into the base.

He picked up something the umpire dropped.

And he cheered for his teammates from the dugout.

48

In the ninth inning, the score was tied and Frankie was on third base. One of Frankie's teammates hit the ball high into the outfield.

Frankie ran to home plate and
scored the winning run!

After the game, the teams high-fived each other and said, "Good game!"

Frankie ran to the umpire, **shook his hand** and **thanked him** for calling the game.

Another player even came up to
Frankie to tell him he made a good play.

Frankie's family congratulated him.
"Well played!" "We're proud of you!"

As they were leaving, Jason ran up to Frankie.
"You were right. I was being a bad sport.
I'm sorry for taking away from the fun.
Thank you for being a good teammate."

Frankie smiled and said,
"Thanks, Jason. I think this is going
to be a great season!"

It felt good to play fair and respect others. Being a good sport made baseball even more fun!

58

THINK TALK ABOUT IT

Discuss the story...

1. What does it mean to show good sportsmanship?

2. How did Frankie show good sportsmanship throughout the story?

3. What does it mean to show bad sportsmanship?

4. What do you think changed Jason's attitude and helped him start showing good sportsmanship?

5. Even though the other team lost, how did the players show good sportsmanship?

Discuss how to apply the story...

1. What sports do you like to play?

2. What would happen if people didn't play with good sportsmanship?

3. Explain a time when someone displayed poor sportsmanship toward you. How did you feel?

4. When you see others displaying bad sportsmanship, what is a kind way you can remind them to be a good sport?

5. What are some ways you can show good sportsmanship to the other team and game officials?

FOR PARENTS & MENTORS: *Good sportsmanship makes a big difference for all who are involved in the game, from players and coaches to parents and spectators. As a parent you can model good sportsmanship by how you cheer from the sidelines, allowing the coaches to give direction and interacting well with the game officials. Even watching sports at home can be a good teaching opportunity. Point out players who display good sportsmanship and those who do not. Talk about what a player could have done differently. If a game official makes a call that seems incorrect, explain that is part of the game and the players still need to show respect. Displaying good sportsmanship when the game gets frustrating can be hard, but that's when it matters the most.*

For additional tips and reference information, visit **www.MVPkids.com**.

Meet the
mvpkids

featured in
Block Bad Sportsmanship™
with their families

MIRIAM NASSER

MRS. ALIAA AHMAD
Aunt

MR. JIBRIL AHMAD
Uncle

HALIM AHMAD
Cousin

SETH AHMAD
Cousin

ALIMA AHMAD
Cousin

DR. ABDUL NASSER
"Baba"

MRS. SALMA NASSER
"Mama"

SARA NASSER
Sister

ADAM NASSER
Brother

LUCAS MILLER

LeBRON MILLER

FRANKIE RUSSO

LEO RUSSO

MR. LORENZO RUSSO
"Dad"

MRS. CLAUDIA RUSSO
"Mom"

LORENZO RUSSO, JR.
Brother

CAMILLA ESPOSITO
"Nona"

63

MVP Kids Game Day Ideas

Good sportsmanship makes playing games fun! Practice being a good sport with these games that encourage team building. Play in your backyard or go to the park to make some new friends. Wherever you play, just remember to play by the rules, work together and encourage the other players!

Blindfolded Egg Walk

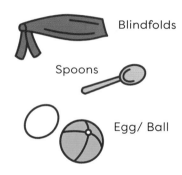

Blindfolds

Spoons

Egg/ Ball

HOW TO PLAY – Determine a starting line and a finish line. One person starts at the starting line, puts on a blindfold and holds the spoon with the egg. Another person uses words to guide the blindfolded person to the finish line.

CHALLENGE – If you have enough people and supplies, make it a race with different teams. You can also add safe obstacles that people will have to navigate around to get to the finish line.

Beanbag Bowl Catch

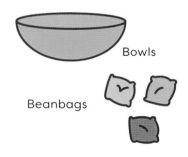

Bowls

Beanbags

HOW TO PLAY – One player holds the bowl above his head. The other player stands several feet away and tries to toss the beanbag into the bowl. The player holding the bowl can move to try to catch the bean bag.

CHALLENGE – Start close together and then after each toss take a step backward. You can also add a rule that the player holding the bowl cannot move his feet, but can only lean his body to try to catch the beanbags.

Balloon Bop

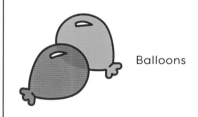

Balloons

HOW TO PLAY – Throw the balloon up in the air and don't let it touch the ground. Keep track of how many times you bop the balloon back up in the air. If it touches the ground, restart counting.

CHALLENGE – Limit which body parts you can use to bop the balloon back up in the air. Take turns selecting either no-hands, head-only, knees-only, etc. (Be careful! Stand far enough away from other players so you don't accidentally bop each other.)

Grow up with our **mvp**kids

CELEBRATE!™
Board Books
Ages 0-6

Our **CELEBRATE**™ board books for toddlers and preschoolers focus on social, emotional, educational and physical needs. Helpful Teaching Tips are included in each book to equip parents to guide their children deeper into the subject of each book.

Celebrate!™
Paperbacks
Ages 4-8

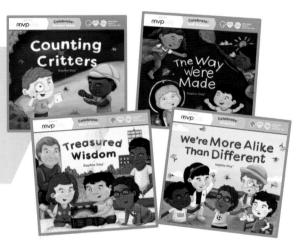

Our **Celebrate!**™ paperback books for Pre-K to Grade 2 focus on social and emotional learning. Helpful Teaching Tips are included in each book to equip mentors and parents. Also available are expertly written, related SEL curriculum and interactive e-book apps.

help **me**
UNDERSTAND™
Elementary
Ages 6-12

Our **Help Me Understand**™ series for elementary readers shares the stories of our MVP Kids® learning to understand and manage specific emotions. Readers will gain tools to take responsibility for their own emotions and develop healthy relationships.

Help your children grow in character by collecting the entire **Help Me Become™** series!

*Our **Help Me Become™** series for early elementary readers tells three short stories in each book of our MVP Kids® inspiring character growth. Each story concludes with a discussion guide to help the child process the story and apply the concepts.*

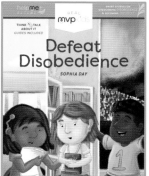

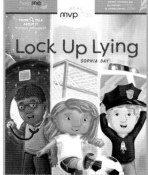

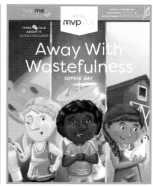

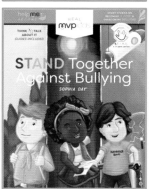

www.mvpkids.com

YONG CHEN

LEO RUSSO

FRANKIE RUSSO

JULIA ROJAS

GABBY GONZÁLEZ

AANYA PATEL

ANNIE JAMES

BLAKE JAMES

SARAH COHEN-GOLDSTEIN